Machine Learning

Table of Contents

Introduction

I would like to thank you for downloading this book.

Machine learning is a sub-field of artificial intelligence. You can say that in this field of study we strive to find better ways to apply AI. The goal behind this field of study is to build intelligent machines—those that are able to learn by themselves.

Arthur Samuel described it back in the 90s as the *"study that gives the ability to the computer for self-learn without being explicitly programmed"*—that means focusing on dynamic algorithms that analyze data and change as new data comes in. You don't need to hard code new actions or pathways because the system itself can develop that on its own.

We know that data grows continually and a lot of it is unstructured, which makes the job of analyzing all of that raw data so laborious and at times excruciating. Studies have shown that 80% of today's data is a cacophony of graphs, documents, photos, videos, and audio. Finding patterns in all of that is a task which has been proven to be impossible for a single human mind.

This is basically one of the major applications of machine learning today—the analysis and computation of massive amounts of data. You can say that because of machine learning technology computers were given a new capability.

And that is the focus of this book. To help you understand what machine learning is in a nutshell. It is assumed that you, the reader, already have some background on related technologies such as computer programming, logic, algorithms, and such. However, you don't need to be so technical to understand the concepts discussed here.

In fact, we have simplified the terms and concepts that even one who doesn't have any programming background can the core concepts of machine learning. We'll go over the details step by step as gently as possible as it were.

Other than going over the different facets of machine learning, you will also learn how to contrast and compare it to different fields of study as well. We'll touch on natural language processing, artificial intelligence, deep learning, and other related studies and how machine learning is similar to and different from them.

The book will also cover the different algorithms used in machine learning according to its different types. We'll cover algorithms for supervised learning, unsupervised learning, and reinforcement learning. In other words we'll go over how machine learning is task driven (e.g. predicting the next value), data driven (e.g. identify and classify customer clusters), and is able to learn from its own mistakes.

We'll also get a bit technical—just slightly when we cover computational learning theory, big data, statistics, learning and optimization, Bayesian networks, support vector machines, genetic algorithms, and data mining. Again, we have tried to the best of our abilities to simplify these concepts for the lay man.

At the end of this book we have also recommended related AI technologies, open source tools, and programming languages. Well, that is if you are interested to learn how to actually develop this technology or to at least be able to understand its more technical features.

Needless to say, machine learning is a new and exciting field with a lot of beneficial applications. It facilitates more accurate medical diagnosis, it can simplify product marketing, create more accurate sales forecasts, improves the precision of many financial rules, simplifies documentation that is time intensive, fine tune predictive maintenance, and a host of other benefits.

May you develop your own insight into the benefits of machine learning in your own field of study. Again, thank you for downloading this book.

Chapter 1. Just What Is Machine Learning (ML)?

Machine learning is everywhere these days. So many people, which may include you and me, are using it dozens of times every day and yet, and some are not even aware of it.

Machine learning has given us effective web search, practical speech recognition, and self-driving cars. It has even improved our understanding of the human genome on a vast scale that scientists are now at the forefront of studying how medicines affect each individual. This means that someday, medicines will be population-specific, or at its best, patient-specific, which is in contrast to today's approach: one-size-fits-all.

The resurgence of interest in machine learning has little to do with making human lives convenient, to say the least. It's slowly becoming popular because many enjoy the ubiquitous home assistants (Amazon Alexa, Google Home, etc.) and superhuman game plays (AlphaGo and Atari with Deep Learning).

Machine learning is increasingly being researched and used due to factors such as affordable data storage, cheaper but more powerful computational processing, and growing varieties and volumes of available data. All of these are popular thanks to Bayesian and data mining analysis. It all has something to do with big data.

All of these factors indicate that it's now possible to create quickly, if not automatically, software, products, devices, and other technology models that can analyze and deliver bigger, more complex, and more accurate data and results. In other words, we can now build more precise models.

But what exactly is Bayesian analysis? What about data mining? We'll get to know more of them in the next chapters as we dig deeper into what machine learning is. Researchers have always believed that the best way to make progress towards human-level AI is to study more about machine learning. First, let's take a look at its basic concepts.

Machine Learning Defined

According to Wikipedia,

> "Machine learning (ML) is the scientific study of algorithms and statistical models that computer systems use to progressively improve their performance on a specific task."

TechTarget meanwhile, defines machine learning as,

> *"a category of algorithm that allows software applications to become more accurate in predicting outcomes without being explicitly programmed."*

But what does this all mean?

Machine learning is a branch of AI, or artificial intelligence. Researchers believe it is a way towards achieving improvements in AI. How?

Machine learning is based on the idea that computer systems, with minimal human intervention, can make decisions using what it has just learned from data and identifying patterns from it as well.

This means that machine learning analyzes data and builds analytical models quickly or automatically based on said data. It's like a training method for machines to learn about what's happening around them and then making a decision based on data it's being given with.

Considering its definition is nearly similar to that of AI, machine learning is always used interchangeably with other AI-related projects and terminologies.

Machine Learning vs. Machine Language

Machine language is not AI. It has however, the word "machine" attached to it. While not all words with "machine" on them can be used interchangeably with machine learning, machine language has been used as so because it shares a common denominator: computer systems. But what's the difference?

Machine learning is all about "telling" or "asking" machines to accomplish certain tasks without the need to "teach" them how to at first. Computer systems therefore, do not need to be explicitly programmed prior to giving it instructions. They do what they have to do based on the data that's been, like mentioned above, given to them.

Machine language, or machine code, on the other hand, is the "mother tongue" of computers. It is composed of digital binary – only 0s and 1s, which is also called low-level language. Programmers, or coders, write programs or software using human-readable text such as Python, Java, C, etc. These are called high-level languages. These programs are converted or compiled into machine-readable forms, or machine language, using an interpreter or compiler so computers can understand them.

Machine Learning vs. Natural Language Processing (NLP)

The truth is, computers are still unable to analyze human communication. We humans use abbreviations, jargons, slang, and colloquialisms all the time. Many don't even bother correcting their misspellings.

Human communication has become too vague for computer analysis. The inconsistencies of natural human language make it difficult to understand. In short, human language is frustrating. Well, at least from computers' point of view.

In the last decade however, and thankfully, machine learning and natural language processing (NLP) have progressed immeasurably. Machine learning uses NLP to provide products and services that can interpret the words that we humans speak or write on computers (or any mobile device) about. Natural language processing studies and develops computer systems that interpret text and speech that we humans naturally use.

Later in this eBook, you will learn more about how machine learning, through various algorithms or methods, uses NLP to analyze spoken and typed or written data.

Machine Learning vs. Artificial Intelligence (AI)

Science fiction novels and Hollywood movies always depict artificial intelligence as robots with human-like features and thinking power that take over the world. The truth is, AI is far from that.

AI technologies and its current evolution isn't that smart (yet) or even scary. Instead, AI is ever-changing and improving to provide many industries with specific benefits.

Machines that perform tasks with human intelligence characteristics are considered AI. To do so, AI includes tasks such as understanding language, recognizing sounds and objects, learning, planning, and problem solving. Machine learning, at its core, is simply a way of accomplishing these tasks; it's simply a way to achieve AI.

To make it short, AI can be used without machine learning, although that would mean hard-coding, or a programmer has to create millions of lines of codes using complex decision-trees and rules. Machine learning therefore, makes AI easier. There's less hard coding because machines are "taught" to improve or adjust themselves based on a situation, instruction, or data.

Machine Learning vs. Deep Learning

There are many approaches to machine learning. There are Bayesian networks, reinforcement learning, clustering, inductive logic programming, decision tree learning, and many more. Deep learning is also one of them.

Deep learning is an aspect of AI that enables systems to gain certain types of human knowledge by "learning" how we learn. According to scientists, it is comparable to a way of automating predictive analytics. To accomplish this, deep learning has to have characteristics of the human brain, which it now has.

In fact, deep learning was inspired by the interconnecting neurons in the human brain. It uses algorithms that work similarly with the biological structure of the human brain. These algorithms are called Artificial Neural Networks (ANNs).

ANNs are huge neural networks containing deep and vast layers of processing units from which its name has been derived from. Each layer of processing units, or neurons, has its own task – pick up or learn individual, complex data such as edges or curves in image recognition, or words in speech recognition.

What are Machine Learning Tasks?

As mentioned earlier, machine learning takes vast amount of data as input. Each of its algorithms however, aims to achieve different tasks. Algorithm in computer science is a broad term used to describe processes or sets of rules that should be followed to solve a problem. In Chapter 3 of this eBook, you'll get to know more about these algorithms.

For now, machine learning algorithms can be broadly classified based on the common tasks they are designed to solve. These tasks are: clustering, regression, and classification.

Clustering

Groups of data are called clusters and the task of creating these groups is called clustering, which happens fully automatically. This task finds natural groups of data and a label that is associated with each of these groups. Common examples include product features identification and customer segmentation.

To achieve clustering, some of the common machine learning methods used are:

- Mean-shift (Higher accuracy)
- Topic models
- K-means
- Hierarchical clustering

Regression

Regression tasks estimate numerical values, also called continuous response variable, by predicting their value. Sometimes, numerical values have to be predicted as is in the case of businesses. What is the salary of a company's workforce? What are the sales for the next 6 months? What will be the cost of a newly built condo? What is the stock price of a company's share next month? These are examples of the type of problems that regression tasks solve.

To solve regression tasks, here are some of the machine learning methods that can be used:

- Gaussian process regression (Higher accuracy)
- Kernel regression (Higher accuracy)
- LASSO (least absolute shrinkage and selection operator)
- Support vector regression
- Linear regression
- Regression trees

Classification

Classification tasks predict a category of a data, also called discrete variables. For example, if there's a group of pictures with animals and humans in it, animals will be classified as animals and humans will be classified as humans. Machine learning is often used to classify voices, objects, fraud, and diseases in the real world.

To solve classification tasks, machine learning methods that are used include:

- Kernel discriminant analysis (Higher accuracy)
- Random forests (Higher accuracy)
- Support vector machine (SVM) (Higher accuracy)
- Artificial neural networks (ANN) (Higher accuracy)
- K-Nearest Neighbors (Higher accuracy)
- Deep learning

- naive Bayes
- Logistic regression
- Boosted trees
- Decision trees

To continue learning more about machine learning, it's time to take a look back at its history and how it has evolved today.

Chapter 2. History of Machine Learning

We learned earlier that although machines can be potentially scary, they can also be highly intelligent. They can actually, truly learn. Today, computers don't need to be explicitly programmed to learn from data and improve themselves. They simply need algorithms in machine learning.

Machine learning algorithms enable computers to autonomously drive cars, write and publish sport match reports, communicate with humans, and even find terrorist suspects. It's how we can communicate with home assistant devices, or how a super car parks itself, or, how a bank approves (partially) loan requests. Machines are getting increasingly intelligent, enabling AI to expand to more businesses and industries.

In this chapter, this eBook offers a quick trip through time to look at the history of machine learning and its evolution.

A Brief History

In the 1940s, the word "computer" was used to call people working in various technological companies who had intensive numerical computation capabilities. It was also during this decade that ENIAC (Electronic Numerical Integrator And Computer) was invented. It was the first manually operated computer system, making it the first "digital" computer. The idea behind its conception was to build a machine that can imitate human thinking and learning. All along, the plan was to create machines that can think and learn the way humans do.

By the next decade, Perceptron was invented. It was an algorithm that acts as a linear classifier intended to classify data input. That may have sounded simple, but it has the ability to classify and combine data in large numbers. It became a powerful tool in computing. It was a real breakthrough.

There were many more research and discoveries in machine learning in the next 20 years. However, there were several years of stagnation beginning in the 1980s. Thanks to the intersection of statistics and computer science, machine learning gained popularity again in 1990s.

The 90s can be considered as the first golden age of machine learning. The use of statistics in computer science and statistics created probabilistic approaches and prediction analytics in artificial intelligence. This shifted AI towards data-driven approaches. Because there were large-scale data available, scientists were able to build intelligent systems that can learn and analyze from large amounts of data.

Aside from developing powerful algorithms, scientists were also able to build better hardware and the technology. Computers have become smaller, more manageable, and portable. The progress continued into the 21st century as we enjoy the concept of Deep Learning today.

The Genesis

So, when did machine learning came into the picture? Alan Turing in 1950 asked the question,

> *"Can computers think?"*

in his academic journal, Mind, published in October 1950. He subsequently developed the Turing Test which attempted to measure the performance or "intelligence" of computers. Nine years later, Arthur Samuel first used the term "machine learning" to describe how a computer game program he developed, Checkers, can learn as it ran, improving its ability to beat human opponents.

A Detailed Timeline and the Current Status of Machine Learning

Google divided the developments made by machine learning and its timeline into three eras:

1. The Groundwork from 1642 to 1936
2. Theory to Reality from 1943 to 1999
3. Modern Machine Learning from 2006 to present

However, we'll focus on machine learning's more recent developments.

The Groundwork

The truth is, many of the underpinnings of modern machine learning have something to do with mathematical operations and equations. They all predate computers and could have started with the advent of mechanical calculators in 1642 and the invention of the binary system in 1647.

However, it was the creation of Least Squares method in 1805, the definition of Bayes' Theorem in 1812, and the development of the Markov Chains in 1913 that laid the foundation for modern machine learning.

Theory to Reality

In the late 1940s, manually-operated computers were developed to hold their programs (instructions) in the same memory used for data. These machines included:

- Manchester Small-Scale Experimental Machine (1948)
- The Manchester Mark 1 and Cambridge's EDSAC (1949)
- University of Pennsylvania's EDVAC (1951)

This began the modern computing revolution.

In 1951, the first artificial neural network was built by Marvin Minsky and Dean Edmonds. It was a computer-based simulation of the way how human brains work.

The term 'machine learning' was first used in 1959. It was coined by Arthur Samuel, a pioneer in artificial intelligence and computer gaming. Machine learning was a scientific venture that stemmed from a quest for artificial intelligence. Back then, researchers wanted to make machines learn data. So, they tried to use symbolic methods and neural networks.

Neural networks are algorithms that have been loosely modeled after the human brain. They are meant to recognize patterns and interpret sensory data via labeling, clustering, or machine perception. They recognize patterns that are numerical and contained in vectors.

However, in the 1960s through 1980s, people became disappointed when there weren't any more breakthroughs and so funding for machine learning and AI research were reduced dramatically. The highlight came when in 1996, Deep Blue, an IBM computer, beat Garry Kasparov, world champion in chess. Once again, machine learning gained traction.

Modern Machine Learning in the 21st Century

Today, some of the most recent developments in ML include:

- Microsoft Kinect (2010)
- IBM Watson (2011)
- GoogleBrain (2012)
- AlexNet (2012)
- DeepFace by Facebook (2014)
- DeepMind by Google (2014)
- OpenAI by Elon Musk (2015)
- Amazon Machine Learning Platform (2015)
- ResNet by CNN (2015)
- U-net by CNN (2015)

Chapter 3. Types of Machine Learning

Today, machine learning is used in a variety of applications and industries. For instance, it is widely used in agriculture, economics, linguistics, speech recognition, search engines, computer networks, medical diagnosis, marketing, insurance, and data quality.

The implementation of its algorithms is necessary for maintaining competitiveness. Such implementation also requires resources and strategic steps. Hence, it is vital to determine your purpose for using machine learning. You also have to understand the different types of machine learning algorithms and their benefits.

Keep in mind that the different types of machine learning algorithms solve different types of problems. If you combine these algorithms, you can effectively deal with various tasks as well as obtain valuable information. Nearly everything benefits from machine learning algorithms, the most ubiquitous of which is social media apps.

Terminologies to Remember

When it comes to machine learning, you have to learn and understand specific terminologies such as labeled data, classification, and regression.

Labeled data refers to the data that consists of training examples. These examples are pairs that feature inputs and desired output values, which are known as supervisory signals or labels.

Classification refers to the prediction of discrete values, such as true or false.

Regression refers to the prediction of continuous values, such as prices.

The Different Types of Machine Learning Algorithms

Machine learning algorithms generally differ in approach, data type, and purpose. It is necessary for you to figure out the type of data that you wish to input or the type of problem that you want to solve before you select an algorithm. The following are the primary categories of machine learning algorithms:

Supervised Machine Learning Algorithms

These are the ones that require direct operation supervision. The sample data corpus is labeled and strict boundaries are set. In essence, it is a spoon-fed version. You choose the type of data output or samples that you give the algorithm. You also see the type of result that you want. The machine views the process as a routine of connecting dots.

Supervised learning is primarily meant to determine the scope of data. It is also meant to make predictions of unseen, unavailable, or future data based on labeled sample data. In Chapter 5, we will discuss this a bit more.

Regression and classification are the two main processes of supervised machine learning. Regression refers to the process of calculating outcome predictions and identifying patterns. The system needs to process numbers, values, and grouping among others

Classification refers to the process in which the incoming data is classified based on previous data samples. It manually trains algorithms to recognize object types as well as categorize them properly. The system needs to know how to distinguish the different classes of information as well as perform a binary, optical character, or image recognition.

The most commonly used supervised algorithms include linear regression, random forest, logistical regression, gradient boosted trees, neural networks, support vector machines, decision trees, nearest neighbor, and naïve bayes.

A support vector machine is a supervised machine learning algorithm that can be used for regression and classification challenges. A decision tree has a tree-like model of decisions, including their possible consequences, outcomes, utility, and costs.

Naïve bayes is a simple algorithm that can be applied to data. It makes assumptions since every variable in the dataset is naïve. It is used to obtain the dataset's base accuracy.

Usually, supervised learning is used in trend forecasting and price prediction. It is used to make forecasts in stocks, sales, and retail commerce. Algorithms use incoming data to evaluate possibilities as well as calculate possible results.

You can think of it as a concept of function approximation in which algorithm is trained and the function that most accurately describes the input data is chosen.

Oftentimes, people have a hard time figuring out the real function that makes the right predictions. The algorithms also tend to rely on the assumptions made by humans with regard to how computers should learn. This results in a bias.

Humans act as teachers that feed computers with training data. Patterns are then learned from such data. Supervised learning algorithms model the dependencies and relationships between input features and target prediction outputs.

Unsupervised Machine Learning Algorithms

These are the ones that do not have any direct developer control. They are the opposite of supervised machine learning algorithms, which allow users to sort out data and identify results. With unsupervised machine learning algorithms, the results remain unknown and unlabeled data is used.

Unsupervised machine learning algorithms are used to explore information structure, extract useful insights, detect patterns, and implement patterns into operations. Essentially, they sift through information in order to make sense of it.

K-means clustering and association rules are common algorithms in unsupervised machine learning. They are often used in campaigns, marketing, and merchandising. Clustering searches for inherent and natural structures among objects. Association rules, on the other hand, identify interesting relationships between objects in massive commercial databases.

Clustering and dimensionality reduction are used by unsupervised learning algorithms to describe data. With clustering, data is explored and segmented into clusters or groups based on internal patterns with no previous knowledge of their group credentials. Such credentials are evaluated by the similarity of individual data objects as well as aspects of their dissimilarity.

Incoming data typically has lots of noise and dimensionality reduction is used to remove them while retaining valuable information. The algorithms that are most commonly used include k-means clustering, associative rule, principal component analysis (PCA), and t-distributed stochastic neighbor embedding (t-SNE).

Unsupervised learning in ad tech and digital marketing are typical. Algorithms are also applied to adjust services and explore customer data. Then again, lots of "known unknowns" are present in the incoming data. A business operation's effectiveness relies on its ability to understand unlabeled data as well as obtain valuable insights from it.

Semi-Supervised Machine Learning Algorithms

They represent the middle ground between unsupervised and supervised algorithms. They feature certain aspects of both algorithms and combine them. In most practical situations, their cost to label is high because expertise is required.

Hence, semi-supervised algorithms are ideal for model building. Through these methods, it is believed that vital information regarding group parameters is carried by an unlabeled data.

Semi-supervised machine learning algorithms employ limited labeled sample data in order to obtain the operation requirements. Such limitation yields a partially trained model that eventually makes the task label an unlabeled data. The results are called pseudo-labeled because they have a limited sample data set.

Both pseudo-labeled and labeled data sets are then combined to create a unique algorithm that features predictive and descriptive aspects of unsupervised and supervised learning.

Semi-supervised learning is typically used in healthcare and legal industries. It is also used in content aggregation systems and crawling engines. It makes use of different labels for the analyzation of content as well as its arrangement in certain configurations.

Reinforcement Machine Learning Algorithms

The idea behind reinforcement learning is to understand machine learning artificial intelligence. It is mainly about the development of self-sustained systems that improve themselves based on the combination of incoming data interactions and labeled data. It also involves trial and error.

Reinforced machine learning uses a strategy known as exploitation or exploration. It is pretty straightforward in its purpose – execute the action, observe the consequences, and take another action that is based on the previous one.

Algorithms are also regarded as reward signals that show up when certain tasks are done. These signals serve as navigation equipment for reinforcement algorithms. It is important to have them because they determine whether or not an action is right.

There are two types of reward signals: positive and negative. The positive ones encourage and promote the continuous performance of a certain series of actions. The negative ones penalize for doing certain actions. They urge to correct such algorithms to avoid being penalized again.

Then again, you have to take note that the functions of reward signals may still depend on the nature of information. Your reward signals may be classified based on the operation's requirements too. In other words, the system minimizes negative rewards while maximizing positive ones.

The most commonly used reinforcement learning algorithms are q-learning, Monte Carlo tree search, temporal difference, deep adversarial, and asynchronous actor-critic agents.

Q-learning refers to the value-based reinforcement learning algorithm that is used to search for the best action-selection policy via the Q function. Temporal difference learning is a learning approach that predicts quantity based on future values. Its algorithms are usually used to predict the measure of the total amount of future rewards.

Reinforcement learning algorithm is also commonly referred to as the agent. It frequently learned from its environment until it learned from its own experiences. It is also called Artificial Intelligence since it allows software agents and machines to instantaneously identify their ideal behavior in just a short period of time.

Furthermore, you have to provide a simple reward feedback. This way, your agent can adapt to and adopt your behavior. When this happens, you can call it a reinforcement signal. Remember that there are tons of different algorithms that you can check out to deal with issues.

In fact, reinforcement learning is determined by specific problems. Its solutions are also called reinforcement learning algorithms. When a step is repeated to solve a problem, such problem becomes a Markov Decision Process.

If you want to produce intelligent programs or agents, you have to observe your input state, use a decision making function to perform a certain action, and receive a reinforcement or reward for performing the action. The state-action pair information regarding your reward also gets stored.

It is possible to use a variety of criteria to identify the different types of machine learning algorithms. Nevertheless, it may be better to use a learning task that visualizes the entire picture of machine learning.

Chapter 4. Machine Learning and its Relationship to Other Fields

Machine learning is related to various fields in computer science and mathematics. Delving into machine learning often requires a familiarity, and in some cases, in-depth knowledge of this field.

Machine learning is related to data mining, optimization, and statistics among others. It uses the same methods as data mining; but instead of focusing on the discovery of unknown properties, it focuses on predictions based on known properties.

Likewise, it shares characteristics with optimization. However, instead of minimizing the loss on training sets, its algorithms minimize the loss on unseen samples. Furthermore, it is related to statistics in the sense that its ideas, including its theoretical tools and methodological principles, have had long been connected to statistics. There have also been several statisticians who used machine learning as basis for their methods.

Here's a closer look at some of the fields often used together and, sometimes, confused with machine learning.

Machine Learning and Data Mining

Data mining is the method of learning patterns or extracting knowledge from extensive amounts of data. The process transforms seemingly random and raw information into something useful for those using it. The result of the process would provide software programs, data scientists, or decision-makers a prediction of the future based on the data analyzed.

Data mining uses data pre-processing, data management processes, model and inference considerations, complexity considerations, interestingness metrics, online updating, visualization, and post-processing of discovered structures. The overlap of methodologies between computer science and statistics makes it an interdisciplinary sub-field of the two disciplines.

One application of data mining is in healthcare. It can analyze the data collected from various hospitals and clinics. It can then provide a prediction of future demand so that decision-makers can create effective decisions in allocating equipment and healthcare personnel between different locations.

Another application is in retail. Data on consumer purchases can be mined to help retailers create more effective promos and store layouts.

However, data mining cannot learn from the patterns it sees from the data collected. It can only provide information for further use and would need human interaction for application. This is where machine learning differs from data mining as it does not need human interaction to teach itself and apply what it learns on its own.

This does not mean that data mining cannot be used in machine learning. In fact, machine learning uses the input provided by data mining for creating models. These models are then used in predicting future outcomes and in creating a foundation for further learning.

Machine Learning and Optimization

Optimization, also known as mathematical programming or mathematical optimization, is the selection of the best (most optimal) solution from the available alternatives while considering a given set of variables. The "best element" is not limited to only one input values as it most often can be a variety of variables.

Real life applications of optimization can be seen in manufacturing where it is used to determine project scheduling, assembly scheduling, and assembly line configurations. It is also used in finance to optimize portfolios, match and time trades, and manage cash.

In retail, it is used to optimize inventory for demand and profitability, planning inventory replenishment, and optimizing store layout and inventory. In logistics, it is used in timetabling, container management, crew scheduling, and airport resources allocation.

Machine learning uses optimization during the training phase where parameters are selected in order for a given function to be optimized. Some topics under mathematical optimization commonly used in machine learning include continuous optimization, stochastic optimization, constrained optimization, and dynamic programming.

However, the use of these topics does not mean that mathematical optimization and machine learning are looking for the same type of solution. Optimization seeks to maximize/minimize the gain/loss on a training set while machine learning is only concerned with minimizing losses on future samples of data.

Machine Learning and Statistics

Statistics is a branch in mathematics that deals with collecting, organizing, analyzing, interpreting, and presenting data. It uses a data set known as a statistical population or statistical model in achieving the objectives of a statistical study. Due to its purely mathematical nature, statistics only aims to see correlations and insights in the data.

Some of its real-world applications include creating models that show consumer behavior on certain seasons of the year, and foot and road traffic on a given location.

Machine learning uses statistics to collect and interpret the data it has available. Machine learning would not be able to make sense of the given data without statistics. Moreover, machine learning resulted from statistics' various methodological principles and theoretical tools.

Although both fields can provide a predictive model, statistics and machine learning are two different fields. First, machine learning is used to create an algorithm that can predict the future while statistics is limited to creating a mathematical model that gives a description and pattern of the data. Second, machine learning uses a combination of fields including computer science and mathematics while statistics is only limited to mathematics. Lastly, machine learning is used to create hypotheses while statistics is used to see data correlations, multivariable, and univariates.

Machine Learning and Big Data

Big data analytics, or simply Big Data, is the collection and analysis of large amounts of data sets for creating useful information in decision-making. For data to be qualified as Big Data, it should have extreme volume, wide variety, and processed at a high rate. This field involves data capture, data processing, data storage, data analysis, visualization, querying, security, and sharing.

Big data is used in healthcare to identify patterns in drug side effects, opportunities for cost reduction, and more effective treatments of certain health conditions. It is also used in manufacturing to forecast output, track defects in processes, increase efficiency of energy use, and simulating new processes.

Big data is used to get the data inputs machine learning needs to create and verify its algorithms. Although it can provide analytical functions, data scientists can only do mathematical models in Big Data. For creating algorithmic models, Big Data needs the capabilities of machine learning.

Chapter 5. Replicating Human Learning in Machines: An introduction to Computational Learning Theory

Artificial intelligence (AI) is much closer to our everyday lives than you might expect. Apple's Siri and Microsoft's Cortana are not the only evidences of computer intelligence that pervade our everyday lives. The handy Google search engine with its predictive text feature, the Facebook posts preference system in your social media feed and the product recommendations that you viewed in your last online shopping spree are all products of AI technology.

More specifically, they are the outcomes of the research made under a branch of AI, Machine Learning and of its specific theoretical branch, Computational Learning.

AI and Machine Learning

Remember that artificial intelligence is a broad umbrella term for the scientific studies which aim for the improvement and innovation of computers and machines to enable them to develop capabilities that mimic that of human beings. A specific branch of AI that aims to discover how machines could be made and modified to learn as human beings do is called Machine Learning.

Machine learning research aims to replicate the human learning processes that we use in our everyday lives in the algorithms that they put into computers and other machines, which scientists and researchers call "learners". These algorithms, or the sets of rules that direct the program embedded in the machines, modify the learners' behavior in response to the stimulus of its environment and its experiences.

Let's take a look back at the supervised learning process which was discussed in a previous chapter. Machine learning makes use of supervised learning, where an algorithm is made with given data samples that are labelled according to their utility in the current learning task of the machine or computer the "learners".

The algorithm then places the samples in a classifier, which is a function that enables the assignment of labels and categories to the data samples, even those that have not yet been encountered before by the learner.

The end-goal of the supervised learning paradigm is to optimize the performance of the learner so that it will get minimal mistakes in handling new samples of data.

Computational Learning Theory and the Principles behind It

Often, machine learning and the computational learning theory itself, is bound and presented together as one and the same. They aren't. Computational learning theory is in fact considered as a sub-branch of not only machine learning but also of artificial intelligence and statistics.

Since it is under machine learning, computational learning theory is all about the *design* and *analysis* of the learning algorithms that are used by machines and computers. The field focuses on trying to understand how man and eventually, the machines, fundamentally learn rules and patterns from data through computational processes.

The foundational principles that govern the computational learning theory are based on the cognitive or mental processes that we human beings go through when we learn about the world around us and our experiences. Similar to human beings, machines are given learning tasks in particular environments, such as those available in marketing or in business, etc. The learners are then designed to learn from the stimuli in these environment and their experiences, which in turn, will become parts of their data. Afterwards, they will form or adapt their algorithm for rules and guidelines that would inform present and future decisions and applications that the learner-machine would encounter.

Aside from this, researchers of the theory also concern themselves with creating algorithms that could supplement the computational limits of computers and machines as learners. Computer scientists push computational learning further so that their learners could learn various kinds of tasks in different environments more successfully. After working on the basic algorithms, they expect the learners to learn from the data they gathered and improve their performance through feedbacking systems.

Looking closer at processes and developments

At present, the learning algorithms used in computational learning are commonly used for predictive and computational efficiency. As stated above, similar to human learners, computer scientists working under the theory are working on the key aspects of learning that should be imbibed well in the machine-learners: how they interact with the experiences in the learning environment, the successful completion of the learning tasks, and optimizing the efficiency of the learners' data usage and processing time.

Since computational learning is modeled after human learning, much of the theoretical learning models used for computer and machine algorithms are abstracted from real life. The experimental scientists then make use of this real-life abstract information to innovate the theoretical and predictive performance of the learners. For them, a good theoretical model that works well for the learners would be a simple one that is able to adapt well in various scenarios and can create insights from the gathered experiential data.

One of the highlighted progress when it comes to computational learning theory is the machine learners' ability to quickly learn and analyze massive amounts of information despite distractions. The designers of the programs under the theory can then readily input more information, even double the previous amount, into the learners with minimal possible damage to the learners' existing algorithm.

Everyday advantages and uses in various fields

Most of the current everyday uses and practical advantages that are provided by computational learning are greatly apparent in the predictive and computational processes needed in big data, which require computational analysis.

For example, computational learning theory could help businesses crunch quickly and accurately big data in order to predict market trends and more profitable opportunities.

It also has applications in sales and marketing. The creation of a more personalized shopping experience and virtual assistance could be made possible by the learners' analysis of consumer habits and preferences

In health and medicine, data collection and analysis can help identify the status of the patients in order to improve treatments and diagnosis

Computational learning could provide valuable aid to travelers as it can provide information such as the best travel routes by providing needed information like traffic status updates and best tourist spots, etc.

Chapter 6: Artificial Neural Networks

The human brain is such a powerful computer. One of its really impressive strengths is in field of pattern recognition. The brain receives input from the environment, and then it then categorizes all the information, and finally it generates an output.

Now, that is the not the most amazing thing about it. The really mind blowing thing is that it does all that in a fraction of a second with little effort involved.

Here's a quick example to demonstrate that. Look at the picture below:

I bet it didn't take you a second to recognize all the numbers from 0 to 9. That's how fast your brain did all the work.

This pattern recognition system is the very same one you use to determine if another person is angry or maybe displaying another emotion. It is a completely involuntary work—you see the expressions you interpret accordingly. This automatic system kicks in via our perceptions and also through our fears.

So, what has that got to do with Artificial Neural Networks? Well, everything. The goal behind the creation of artificial neural networks is to make a computer mimic well at least to some degree that ability.

Artificial Neural Network Defined

An artificial neural network (ANN) is a model or system in computer science that mimics biological neural networks. In simpler terms, you are teaching a computer how to think and analyze things the way the human brain does.

Well, you're trying to do that to a certain degree at least. There's currently no way for us to completely mimic the functions and the processes of the human brain. It's just way too complex.

A Short History of ANN

ANN's history starts way back in 1943 when Walter Pitts and Warren McCulloh used threshold logic to create a mathematical model that mimics a neural network. What they started became the basis for two approaches in this area of research. The first one focused on how to apply ANN to artificial intelligence. The other one focused on finite automation or the creation of finite state machines.

There were problems encountered in the development of ANN, of course. Years later D. O. Hebb creates Hebbian learning or unsupervised learning which we covered in chapter 3 of this book. The exclusive-or problem was then solved in 1975 via Werbo's backpropagation algorithm.

Support vector machines became more popular for quite a bit after that. Of course, part of the research was slowed down due to limited computing power at the time. That eventually changed as better hardware i.e. more powerful GPUs were created.

Better technology paved the way for ANNs to be deployed over a large scale. It also allowed for better visual recognition and image processing. And then later technologies such as deep learning and convolutional networks came around.

How Does an ANN Work?

We can say that an ANN mimics the brain at solving particular problems—well loosely mimicking to be exact. For one thing, it needs input fed to it unlike the biological brain that can take any input directly from the environment.

It is called an "artificial" neural network simply because the neurons are artificial or theoretical. These artificial neurons are at the core of this technology that allows a computer to recognize patterns.

For instance, there are artificial neurons that take in several input, process them, and then creates a single output. The most basic type of artificial neuron is called the perceptron.

Perceptrons and Weighted Inputs

The perceptron was developed by Frank Rosenblatt back in the late 1950s. His work was inspired by model created by McCulloh and Pitts. We use more sophisticated neural networks today but they all still follow the same principles for perceptrons.

A perceptron will take binary inputs, process them, and it will produce a binary output. It doesn't seem much but that's basically how fundamental decision making works. Let's take a look at a simple yet practical example.

Let's say you usually walk to the office to work but you also have the option to work from home. You usually work in the office during workdays and when it isn't raining. On rainy or snowy days you stay at home and just send your work online.

So let's say further that you want to create an algorithm that will decide whether you have to go to the office or just stay home. You will then take all of the aforementioned factors (i.e. what day it is and the weather condition) and use them to compute or solve for the answer to that question.

Since a perceptron only takes binary numbers, 1 would mean yes and 0 would mean no. The variables are day of the week or $x1$ and weather condition or $x2$. So let's say the data is Tuesday and the weather is fine. That'll be a vote of 1 and 1 equals 2, which is a definite answer of yes you're going to walk to the office today.

Let's say the input is Sunday and it's raining. That's 0 + 0 equals 0, which means you're not going to the office today. It's simple so far but it can get complicated when the values of the variables get mixed up.

Let's say it's Wednesday and it's raining. That translates to 1 + 0 equals to 1. That means you're still going to the office. But how different is that from Saturday and sunny? That's still 0 + 1 = 1. So do you go to the office on a rainy Wednesday and still go to the office on a sunny Saturday? There should be a distinction made.

At all costs you're not supposed to be at the office on a Saturday regardless of weather conditions, right? It's your day off—time for yourself. But you still can get to the office to work on a Wednesday even though it's raining—just bring an umbrella or drive to work.

So, how do you make your algorithm make this distinction? How do you make a computer understand that Saturdays and Sundays are your days off?

Well, you don't have to make a computer understand the essence of a day off. But you can make Saturdays and Sundays more meaningful when it comes to decision making. That is accomplished in ANNs using weights. Think of them as some kind of force multiplier. The bigger the weight on a certain variable the more important it is.

Another deciding factor is a threshold value. When the algorithm computes the decision to go to work or not, the result of the process should be either above or below a threshold value. In effect, you're saying yes or no—again, perceptrons only work with binary numbers.

So let's say the weather condition will have a weight of 2 and the day of the week has a weight multiplier of 6. Let's set the threshold value at 5—that means anything less than 5 is a no anything 5 or higher is yes.

That means a rainy Wednesday will be weightier or more important so you go to work and a sunny Saturday won't be much weightier since it's you're day off. Let's put that into numbers, shall we.

Here's the formula we're going to use:

$Y = (\text{day of the week x weight}) + (\text{weather x weight})$

A rainy Wednesday would be:

$Y = (1 \times 6) + (0 \times 2)$

The answer is 6 for a rainy Wednesday. That's definitely a yes.

What about a sunny Saturday? Here is the formula for that:

$Y = (0 \times 6) + (1 \times 2)$

The answer for sunny Saturday is 2, which gives us the answer of no; you're not going to work today even if it is bright and sunny.

And that is how a perceptron does the math when it makes decisions. This computation is called a linear combination and the example we have above is very simple. The more complex algorithms use more complicated math. We just made things a lot simple so that regular folks who don't do that much math will understand.

Training a Neural Network

In practice the weights and the other values are actually random. An ANN will actually go through all the random inputs that are fed to it and it will adjust according to the outputs that it will come up with. The neural network will be programmed to adjust to the errors that will come up during computation. This system is called training an ANN.

In our example above, there is only one node or one stopping point or check point where a decision is computed. In more complex ANNs there is an entire network of nodes where complex computations are done at each node or check point.

In mathematical terms, a linear computation would look like this:

$$output = \begin{cases} 0 \text{ if } \sum_i w_i x_i < threshold \\ 1 \text{ if } \sum_i w_i x_i \geq threshold \end{cases}$$

In this equation, w is for the weight and x is the input. Notice the conditional "if" expression at the beginning. It's a Boolean expression which is used for decision making.

Types of Artificial Neural Networks

There are actually many types of ANNs. Some of them are the following:

- Feedforward ANN: this is the simplest type. It takes inputs via the input layer (first line of neurons where the inputs are fed). The output can then be passed along a line of sub-layers.

- Recurrent Neural Networr: this is a more complex type of ANN where the data is fed forwards along the line and then possibly back to the start of the line or beginning layers of the network.

- Modular ANN: this type is modeled closely to the human brain where there are networks within networks.

There are of course many other types of ANNs like regulatory feedback, radial basis functions, spiking, neocognitrons, and others. This is a huge subject and cannot be tackled in full in just a single chapter.

ANNs are also quite useful in the real world. They are used in fields such as text categorization and classification, named entity recognition, part of speech tagging, question answering and semantic parsing, paraphrase detection, multi document summaries, and language generation to name a few.

Chapter 7. What is Deep Learning?

Deep learning is one method of machine learning that focuses on learning data representations. It is used to learn directly features and tasks from data that could be in the form of audio, image, or text. Its algorithms use multiple nonlinear processing unit layers to cascade data for extract features and transform it, can learn in supervised or unsupervised manners, and learn multiple representations of a labeled data. It also goes by the terms hierarchical learning and deep structured learning.

Deep learning starts by inputting training data that the algorithm will use for processing the raw data. The training data would have labels for the desired output the algorithm would provide. In a process known as feature learning, the training data teaches the deep learning algorithm how to identify the different images, audio, or texts. Once it is trained in identifying the labeled data, the deep learning algorithm can now classify unlabeled images, audio, or texts from raw data into a similarly labeled form of the training data.

History of Deep Learning

Alexey Ivakhenko and Valentin Grigor'evich Lapa introduced the first working algorithm of deep learning in 1965. However, the term "deep learning" would only emerge in 1986 when Rina Dechter used and introduced it in the field of machine learning.

Kunihiko Fukushima would use the first convolutional neural network in developing the first artificial neural network known as Necognitron. This enabled computers to recognize two-dimensional visual patterns. The concepts from his creation would be used in a variety of ways including identifying specific handwritten numbers, and completing images of incomplete handwriting. These further developments would be applied in postal systems to identify handwritten ZIP codes and sorting them accordingly, and in banking for reading handwritten checks.

The stronger graphic processing units introduced in 1999 gave way to the next significant development in deep learning. The newer GPUs provided the faster processing needed to create working models that needed increased computational requirements. Aside from the dramatic improvement in training deep learning algorithms, research and development started in speech recognition. By 2015, the said research would result into Google's speech recognition technology.

New improvements in the hardware on 2009 would see deep learning networks become capable of shortening the training period from weeks to a matter of days. This gave way to more prevalent and sophisticated use of deep learning in different industries.

How Deep Learning Relates to Neural Networks

It is easy to confuse deep learning with artificial neural networks.. This has been the case even for the experts in the field of neural networks when it emerged as a field. This is due to most deep learning models being based on neural networks.

Deep learning and neural networks are both subfields of machine learning. They are both essentially a class of machine learning algorithms but they are two different fields. Deep learning derived the term "deep" due to the high number of hidden layers in its network.

The layers in deep learning models can range from tens to more than a hundred. As for artificial neural networks, its hidden layers only number from two to three.

The amount of hidden layers in a network is crucial for creating the output. More hidden layers translate to more complex features and greater potential for more complicated learning.

Applications of Deep Learning

Providing a personalized layout to customers

The media-services provider Netflix use deep learning algorithms in its internal rating prediction system. This algorithm enabled Netflix to provide individualized movie and show recommendations, and thumbnail images that will encourage subscribers to watch.

If this is done traditionally through A/B testing, it would require an impractical amount of time to create individualized recommendations and layout. Subscribers would get sub-optimal recommendations while the A/B testing is being done. Approaching the solution through deep learning created better video recommendations at a faster rate. Moreover, through the subscriber's watch behavior, the algorithm selected images that are most suitable for the preferences of the users.

Highlight the best photographs

Yelp uses deep learning to highlight the best user-provided photographs for restaurants.

The local-search service Yelp provides a platform wherein local business can get crowdsourced reviews. In browsing through these businesses, users would prefer to see photo highlights of what they are looking for (food plating and ambience if it's a restaurant, or venue space if it's an events place). The number of likes and rate of click-through is not enough for evaluating the photos since these can easily influence factors unrelated to aesthetics.

Yelp created a set of standards in judging the photos submitted by their users and applied it into a deep learning algorithm. For judging the contents of the photo, they used diversification logic and strategic filters to classify the photos and select the most suitable for the business. For judging the photo quality, they used algorithms that recognize and rate depth of field, alignment, and contrast.

Creating human-like language translation

Google uses recurrent neural networks to translate different languages. This approach maps whole input sentences in one language and maps the output of the same sentence from another language. This resulted to more efficient and accurate translation outputs.

How Deep Learning Helps the Field of Cognitive and Brain Development

There was a theory in the early 2000s that deep learning is not something revolution. It was supposedly something that has been a basic part of how our brain works. The criticism to this thought was that the brain lacks the critical function of algorithms. However, a neuroscience study in 2017 by Jordan Guerguiev, T.P. Lillicrap, and B. Richards presented an algorithm that supports this theory.

The researchers created an algorithm modeled after the biological structure of neurons in the brain's neocortex. This area of the brain is the one responsible for one's flexible thought, reasoning, and prediction. The algorithm successfully identified hand-written numbers and showed a similar behavior to deep learning algorithms even though it was modeled after the brain's biology.

Neuroscientists can use this as a new ground for studies to determine the existence of algorithmic operations in the brain. The current knowledge shows promising potential in understanding how biological neural circuits learn.

Criticism of Deep Learning

Deep learning still has its shortcomings despite the current and potential solutions it can provide. The most evident is in its limitations in understanding concepts of hierarchical structures. One can see this in the current shortcomings in language translations.

Another one is that it cannot represent causality despite it being capable of recognizing correlations. This causes some deep learning models to fail such as in the case of the British police system's difficulty to disqualify sand dune photos from being labeled as "nudes".

Lastly, deep learning is used in some critical tasks, self-driving function in cars, that failure can translate to loss of life and property. These tasks in the opinion of some individuals should never be transferred to autonomous computing. They state that this transfer expects the intelligence of computers can keep up with the unpredictability of human nature. It is their belief that this is completely unethical since it places the responsibility on human life away from human hands and onto computational capabilities.

Chapter 8. What is Big Data?

The term has been around for quite some time but '**big data**' still poses quite a bit of confusion regarding its correct meaning. The big data concept is constantly evolving and it has become a driving force for a lot of digital transformation such as data science, artificial intelligence, and the Internet of Things.

We have generated a huge amount of data since the onset of the digital age. Computers and the Internet have captured a lot of data around the world. Big data is the collection of this data and being able to use it to your advantage. It can be used in a lot of areas like businesses.

What is Machine Learning with Big Data?

Big data is powerful but it can even be more useful when combined with intelligent automation. Using massive processing power, machine learning is helping organizations use, analyze, and manage their data with higher success rates than ever possible.

Machine learning capabilities have impacted healthcare in various ways and have helped improve personalizing treatment plans by analyzing diagnostics and patient data.

In retail, machine learning and big data are being used for building relationships with customers by capturing, analyzing, and using data for a more personalized shopping experience done in real time.

In finance, fraud can be prevented through predictive analytics which is done by analyzing historical datasets and coming up with forecasts.

Stiff competition has driven the automotive industry into leveraging big data analytics and machine learning capabilities in improving customer experience, marketing, and operations.

Five Biggest Differences Between Machine Learning and Big Data

- Data Use. Machines learning can be used for technologies like advanced recommendation engines and self-driving cars. Big data can be used for many purposes such as collecting sales data and financial research.

- Learning Foundations. Machine learning learns from existing data and establishes a foundation needed for the self-learning algorithm. Big data analytics extract data from information that already exists in order to come up with emerging patterns which can then be used to shape decision-making processes.
- Recognition of Patterns. Big data analytics can define patterns through sequence analysis and classifications. Machine learning can take this concept a step ahead through the use of the same algorithms being used by big data analytics and learn from collected data automatically.
- Data Volume. Machine learning is more focused on working with small data sets and overfitting can create problems along the way. As the name suggests, big data is able to work with large-scale datasets and large volume data.
- Purpose. Machine learning was designed to learn through trained data and is good for predicting or estimating future results. Big data was designed to keep large data volumes, analyze them, and come up with an emerging pattern.

While machine learning and big data are not related directly, they can do wonders when combined.

Data Exploration

For many reasons, data exploration allows your business to gain value from all sorts of data ranging from common enterprise data sources to streaming machine data and big data.

Data defines your business. It keeps records of your organization's performance and activity. If you want to know more about a business, you should get to know the corporation's data.

To get the data you need, you need to start somewhere. When you explore data, you'll learn about previous events. You can then begin building a data model or data set that can be used to produce a trend, root cause, and other analytic outcomes.

Poking through data can inspire you. It's because you get to find fresh sources or categorize data sources that can be used for a particular analysis or report.

Before you can analyze data, you need to explore it first. Analysis creates correlations between diverse sources, subjects, structures, and vintages. Finding the right combination of these sources is highly dependent on data exploration before you can have a successful data analysis

Search technology has become very efficient in exploring different data types. It's now able to parse data from different structures and formats, allowing open-ended questions that are not confined to predefined data models. Yes. Just like Google.

Business people are not technical data analysts and they should be able to see data via a business-friendly format. Data exploration should be easy and simple.

With technology comes data exploration speed allowing shorter times from usage to adding business value.

Data Preparation

A lot of businesses who were unable to optimize the power of **big data** failed because they lacked a sound data preparation strategy. Data preparation steps should include acquiring, preparing, curating, and managing the company's data assets.

The essential first step is identifying the organization's decision set. It will define the data sets to be used in supporting a decision, how to manipulate the data, and come up with an analytical process that will define the generation of insight. It's like defining the end game first so that data preparation becomes much simpler.

Next is the process of selecting the data sources that are required in supporting the required decisions. You may not be able to predict all the possible data sources needed, you should be able to at least come up with the primary data sources. In turn, this will help you in defining the data types available and the data cleansing that you need to do.

There are several data cleansing technologies out there and you will want one that will not only accommodate the data types you initially defined but also provide a platform that can connect to your current analytic tools. The data preparation tool should be accessible to all so that decisions will be consistent throughout the organization.

Along the way, you will discover additional data sets that can be useful to your project. New data source assessment is an ongoing process and is an essential decision-making factor.

Data analytics technology is fast evolving and you should be able to identity new tools that can help you in producing required insights. These can range from basic statistical tools to applications based on advanced machine learning.

Datasets themselves are ever evolving and dynamic. Data preparation should be done when new data becomes available so that it becomes readily available.

Classification

Big data was born out of the need for a technology that can manage huge data from various sources and come up with pattern analysis. It handles that dreary task of finding accurate and meaningful data from large, unstructured sources.

This makes classification methods and important part of **big data**. Classification is basically categorizing data and putting them into predefined categories.

Using these classification techniques, data that is previously unstructured is transformed into an organized format. Users can then easily access the needed data.

These classification methods can be used on huge transactional databases in providing data services from large volume datasets which users can access. These methods can be achieved by using different classification algorithms.

- Binary Classification. This approach involves grouping into a couple of categories. One good example is classifying a machine's state if it's good or faulty.

- Multi-class Classification. In this approach, you categorize data into more three or more categories. An example will be classifying gene expressions.

- Document Classification. This a multi-class classification method wherein the document being classified is in a text document form.

Machine learning technologies have hit new maturity levels and as an effect, smart organizations have begun changing their **big data** approaches. In many industries, businesses are reshaping their existing infrastructures to make use of and optimize intelligent automation. They are combining existing data with intelligent technologies that improve productivity and the ability to cater to customers.

As technology evolves and more companies embrace the power and usefulness of machine learning and **big data**, we can expect more developments and more success stories. Machine learning and **big data** are here to stay so it's better to dive into them as early as possible.

Chapter 9. What are Support Vector Machines?

A support vector machine is a supervised machine learning algorithm that is often used for regression and classification purposes. It involves the use of the kernel trick to determine the optimal boundary between the predicted outputs of data transformations. It also separates the data based on outputs or labels.

Furthermore, it is based on the idea of identifying the hyperplane, which is a line that linearly classifies and separates data sets into two classes. The distance between a data point and the hyperplane is called the margin. Ideally, you should select a hyperplane with the largest margin between a point and the hyperplane. This would increase your chances of correctly classifying your new data.

The History of Support Vector Machines

The first ever algorithm for pattern recognition was suggested by R.A. Fisher in 1936. Aronszajn developed the Theory of Reproducing Kernels in 1950. Then, the linear classifier known as the perception was created by Frank Rosenblatt in 1957. It was the most basic type of feedforward neural network.

In 1963, Lerner and Vapnik introduced the Generalized Portrait algorithm; and a year later, Chervonenkis and Vapnik improved it. In 1965, Cover tackled large margin hyperplanes in input space as well as sparseness. In the same year, Mangasarian used similar optimization techniques for pattern recognition.

In 1968, Smith introduced slack variables for overcoming nonseparability and noise. In 1973, Hart and Duda also tackled large margin hyperplanes in input space. Then, in 1974, Chervonenkis and Vapnik introduced statistical learning theory. Vapnik developed this theory further in 1979. That was when support vector machines were started. In the same year, Tscherwonenkis and Wapnik translated Chervonenkis and Vapnik's book into the German language. An English version was soon produced by Vapnik in 1982.

Eventually, similar works were done by Hassoun, Biehl, and Anlauf. In 1990, the usage of kernels was discussed by Wahba, Girosi, and Poggio. In 1992, Mangasarian and Bennett added to Smith's work about slack variables. A study on support vector machines that closely resembled its most recent form was also presented at the COLT conference in 1992.

Then, in 1995, Vapnik and Cortes introduced the soft margin classifier. The algorithm was also extended to the regression case in The Nature of Statistical Learning Theory. In 1998, papers written by Shawe-Taylor and Bartlett covered the generalization of hard margin support vector machines. Soon after, in 2000, Cristianini and Shawe-Taylor provided statistical bounds regarding the generalization of soft margin algorithms as well as the regression case.

Properties and Applications of Support Vector Machines

Support vector machines are accurate, efficient, and ideal for small datasets. They use a subset of training points. However, they are not ideal for large datasets with a high training time. They are also not very efficient on noisy datasets that have overlapping classes.

Support vector machines also have a wide variety of applications. For instance, they are used for hypertext and text categorization. They can reduce the demand for labeled training instances in transductive and inductive settings.

They can also be used to classify images. According to experimental results, they are able to get higher search accuracy as compared to traditional query refinement methods. Likewise, they are ideal for image segmentation systems.

In addition, support vector machines have the capability to recognize hand-written characters. Their algorithm is also widely used for science. They are used to properly classify proteins as well as perform permutation tests.

Linear and Non-Linear Support Vector Machines

In essence, linear methods can only deal with issues that are linearly separable. Their classification thresholds are linear, such as lines, planes, and hyperplanes. They are easier to implement than non-linear methods. For instance, a hyperplane may be used to separate a problem linearly.

Then again, if you are not able to solve this problem using a linear approach, you can use a non-linear method. Non-linear methods usually involve the application of input dataset transformation. Once the data has been transformed, you can use a linear approach for separation purposes.

Take note of the dataset that you have. If it has a high variance, you may have to add more dataset and reduce features. Then, you can use a non-linear approach for classification purposes. If your dataset has a low variance, you may use a linear model.

What Is Empirical Risk Minimization?

Empirical risk minimization refers to the statistical learning theory principle that defines a set of learning algorithms. It is also used to show the theoretical bounds of their performance.

It's simply about improving accuracy of predictions on an unknown true distribution by minimizing the possible error of predictions on the data obtained from the same distribution.

How to Compute for the SVM Classifier

Computing the SVM classifier has evolved throughout the years. In the past, the quadratic programming problem was reduced. This was the classical approach. Today, however, the coordinate descent and the sub-gradient descent are used.

These modern techniques have been found to be better than the classical approach when it comes to dealing with huge, sparse datasets. The sub-gradient methods are particularly ideal for training examples while the coordinate descent is recommended to be used if the feature space dimension is high.

Implementations of Support Vector Machines in Today's World

At present, support vector machines are used in various industries. Wherever you go, you will surely find something that makes use of support vector machines.

For instance, support vector machines are used for text classification tasks like sentiment analysis, spam detection, and assignment categorization. They are also used for image recognition, as well as color-based classification and aspect-based recognition.

What's more, they are ideal for handwritten digit recognition areas like postal automation services. Support vector machines are commonly used to provide solutions to a wide variety of problems in society.

Chapter 10. Bayesian Networks

Bayesian networks are a Probabilistic Graphical Model type which is used in building models extracted from expert opinion and/or existing data.

Bayesian networks are used for a variety of tasks such as decision making even under uncertainty, time series prediction, reasoning, automated insight, diagnostics, anomaly detection, and outcome prediction. They are probabilistic since Bayesian networks are based on probability distributions and employ existing probability laws.

For example, a Bayesian network can be used to represent the relationships between symptoms and diseases. Given the known symptoms, it can compute probabilities of various diseases that may be present.

Bayesian Networks and Causality

Referring to the disease probability previously mentioned, Bayesian networks can be used to predict causality. You probably have heard of it as cause and effect.

Let's take for example this statement – smoking (A) causes lung cancer (B). We can then derive the following concepts:

- B is the causal effect of A
- The statement is based on probability
- If we change A values, the distribution of B will be affected
- This statement is true in some particular contexts

But you need to understand that association is not equivalent to causation. Consider the following statements:

- Lung cancer and yellow teeth are associated
- Will bleaching teeth reduce lung cancer probability?

Markov Blanket

In machine learning and statistics, the Markov blanket concept states a node inside a graphical model possesses the variables required for it to be protected from other factors in the network. Therefore, a node's Markov blanket can be used to predict that particular node's behavior as well as its children's. Judea Pearl coined this term in 1988.

The values of the children and parents of a node give out information about that particular node when plotted in a Bayesian network. However, in order to properly explain the node in question, the parent nodes also need to be included.

In a Bayesian network, a node's Markov blanket is composed of that node's parents, its children, and also the other parents of those children. But in the Markov random field concept, the set of neighboring nodes is a node's Markov blanket.

Bayesian Statistics

Bayesian statistics is a method of applying the laws of probability to solve statistical problems. It provides mathematical tools that can update beliefs in random events by showing new evidence or data regarding those events.

Basically, Bayesian inference defines probability as the measure of confidence or believability that a person has on a particular event's occurrence. You may have an existing belief regarding an event, but this belief may change in light of new evidence. Bayesian statistics provides an established mathematical method of incorporating prior beliefs and new evidence to come up with what is called posterior beliefs.

Bayesian statistics can make you update your subjective beliefs rationally because of the new data observed.

You may notice that this is in conflict with another statistical inference form known as frequentist or classical statistics. Classical statistics states that probabilities are established by a particular random event's frequency observed in repeated trials over a long time.

Let's take rolling a fair (unweighted) six-sided die as an example. If we do it repeatedly, we'll come up with the observation that each number comes up one-sixth of the time.

When doing statistical inference, or extracting statistical data through probabilistic methods, the Bayesian and frequentist approaches, employ different philosophies.

Frequentist statistics attempts to reduce uncertainty by giving estimates. Bayesian statistics, on the other hand, tries to refine and preserve that uncertainty by updating individual beliefs when new evidence shows up.

Bayesian Inference

Bayesian inference is a method of getting more accurate predictions from given data. It can be really useful if you don't have enough data or at least not as much as you would like or required but you still need to get sharper predictions from it.

Although statisticians and mathematicians praise the Bayesian inference, it's not really mystical or magical. And although the underlying match can become complex, the concepts behind Bayesian inferences are easily accessible.

Basically, Bayesian inference helps you come up with stronger conclusions from given data by factoring in what's already known about the answer.

Let's have a practical example. You're at the movies and another moviegoer accidentally drops a ticket. You want to call the moviegoer and give back the ticket. But the moviegoer's back is turned on you and has long hair. Do you say 'Excuse me miss!' or 'Excuse me, sir'. Given that more women in your area have long hair, you'll assume that the moviegoer is a woman, right?

But what about when the person is lined up at the men's restroom? You'll assume that it's a man with long hair. This use of background knowledge and common sense is done without thinking and Bayesian inference uses this concept by employing mathematical calculations which make the predictions more accurate.

Let's put numbers in the equation. There are 100 people in the movies. 50 are women and 50 are men. Out of the women, 25 have long hair while 25 have short hair. Out of the men, only 2 have long hair and the rest have short hair. There are 25 women and only 2 men with long hair. It's then safe to assume that the moviegoer is a woman.

The probability of something happening is the number of ways an event can happen over the total number of events that can happen. In our cinema dilemma, 50 women divided by a total of 100 moviegoers is 50% or 0.5. The probability of the moviegoer's gender is the same for both men and women. But given the restroom factor, it becomes .02 for women and .98 for men.

Using this example, we can then discuss the 3 major Bayesian inferences.

Conditional probabilities. It answers the question 'What's the probability that the person has long hair if you know she's a woman?'. It's computed just like straight probabilities but only using a subset of examples which meet a given condition.

Joint probabilities. This answers the question 'What's the probability that the moviegoer is a woman with short hair?'. It becomes a two-step process wherein we focus first on the probability that the person is a woman and the probability that she has short hair.

Marginal probabilities. This one answers the question 'What is the probability that the person has long hair?'. To get the answer, we add up all the probabilities and all the ways this can happen.

Bayesian networks employing these inferences can come up with accurate decisions and predictions even with limited data.

Chapter 11: Genetic Algorithms, the Darwinian Metaheuristic

Genetic algorithms are used in both operations research and computer science. It is a metaheuristic that is based on Charles Darwin's theory of natural selection. A metaheuristic refers to a high level procedure or search algorithm or to be more precise a partial search algorithm.

Algorithms of this type rely on operations that are inspired natural processes that also occur in nature. As such they can generate pretty good solutions for a lot of search problems and optimization.

Going Back to Charles Darwin

Darwin once said:

"It is not the strongest of the species that survives nor the most intelligent, but the one most responsive to change."

This quote is truly powerful and it reflects exactly the idea behind genetic algorithms. The approach therefore is to find the fittest data (individuals or species etc.) that will propagate and produce better offspring (i.e. best suited output).

To understand how this algorithm works, we must delve into the notions of natural selection. That way, you can fully grasp the approach that genetic algorithms use when it tries to solve different problems.

Let's put it all in simple terms. We all begin with a population of different individuals. Of course these individuals will form families and later on produce offspring. Of course the offspring inherit some of the characteristics of their ancestors.

Now if the fitness of the parents is better, then they are expected to produce better offspring. In fact, the offspring may surpass the fitness level of the parents thus increasing the probability that their species will survive.

This process will repeat over and over from one generation to the next. So, when will it stop? It stops when the fittest individuals have been found.

Now, think of that in search terms. You have a humongous amount of data that will take decades to process. The idea is to select a variety of solutions and then use the process described earlier to find the solution that best fits the search problem that is being addressed.

Five Phases in Genetic Algorithms

Let's streamline and apply the Darwinian concepts described above into several steps:

1. A population is defined – data is selected or sampled
2. Search functions are created and if possible the best one is determined
3. The selected search function is applied to the sample to find the best fitted data given a certain criteria
4. Better suited or even the best suited data is produced.

That is basically how genetic algorithms flow. Now we can move on to the actual phases in this type of algorithm, which include the following:

1. Initial population
2. Fitness production
3. Selection
4. Cross over
5. Mutation

Now as you can see the phases have parallels in the steps outlined before them. You can say that there is an extra phase but we'll explain why that is in a minute.

Initial Population

The process in a genetic algorithm begins with the initial population (e.g. raw customer data). Each unit in this population has its own parameters. Programmers can use different data types to represent the units in this population. This is the sample or partial data that the algorithm will work with.

Fitness Function

How do you define if a unit or individual is the best fit for certain problems? You create certain parameters in your selection ergo a fitness function. You can gauge the fitness of different units/individuals by scoring them or whatever parameters you would like to use.

Selection Phase

The higher the score of a unit the higher is its chances for getting selected to pair with another equally fit unit. They will then be combined (i.e. the parents) to produce offspring (i.e. a better suited data or solution to the original problem being solved).

Crossover Phase

The crossover phase is considered as the most significant step or phase in a genetic algorithm. This is the extra step as you may have observed above. A crossover is made when offspring are created from the parent data or solution. You can think of this as an internal search or fine tuning of the data or solution in order to produce better offspring.

For instance, the parent units are solutions to a problem. We all know that solutions have their pros and cons. A cross over point is selected where features/characteristics/data from the parents and taken and spliced together.

That way there is a better chance to spot the pros and retain them and get rid of the cons from both the parents. This goes back to natural selection again—virtually speaking the offspring is the result of the exchange of characteristics that will be inherited from the two parents. And that is why the offspring is a lot better suited for survival compared to its ancestors because it gets the best from both sources.

Mutation Phase

Some offspring will be subjected to mutation when they are created. The selection of which offspring will be mutated is based on very low random probability. But why do that?

The goal for this step is to maintain diversity and also to prevent the occurrence of a premature convergence—remember we're pairing off units, which rapidly decimates the population. Note that the least fit units will then be replaced by the offspring which are better fit for the problem being addressed.

The following is a flowchart of the different phases in a genetic algorithm:

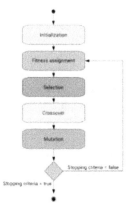

Applications of Genetic Algorithms

There are a lot of applications of genetic algorithms and it is quite useful in different fields. The process that we described above has a direct application to feature selection. You will search from different models and select their feature importance. That way you select features that are most relevant in the prediction of a target variable.

Here are a few real world applications of genetic algorithms:

- *Shipment Routing and Traffic Management*: genetic algorithms can be used to test and recommend the most optimal traffic schemes and shipment routes depending on changing traffic data. The goal of course is to save time and also make transport and logistics more economical.

- *Engineering and Design*: genetic algorithms are already in use in engineering and structural design. This technology is used to simulate the design process and test for sturdiness, economy, and efficiency.

- *Robotics*: another fine example of the application of genetic algorithms is in the construction of learning robots. Some have envisioned them as being able to learn day to day tasks that we humans do.

- *Optimized Telecoms*: this is something like traffic routing—the big difference is that it is applied to telephony systems. The goal is to improve internet performance and better call routing. The goal is for the algorithm to anticipate telecom problems and provide solutions such as the routing of cell towers and their future placement to provide ease of switching and better coverage.

Chapter 12. Machine Learning Applications in Different Sectors and Industries

Machine Learning is a science about how computer systems can improve their performance on specific activities using algorithms and statistics. Since the computer is continuously learning, it accumulates information everyday on what works and what does not work.

For businesses and different industries, applying this technology can make the work more efficient. It can eliminate mundane tasks that slow down productivity. It also measure results. This means you can see exactly how much impact it has on the industry. Here is the machine learning applications in different industries and sectors around the world.

1. Telecommunications

We are now living in a mobile world where it is estimated that 5 billion people have mobile phones. Machine learning for the telecommunication industry means the computer can handle customer service questions, track orders, mobile usage, and troubleshooting just to name a few.

2. Adaptive Websites

These are websites that can change the information on the site as well as the design and presentation to better serve the user. Instead of having one website design for everyone, they have multiple versions of the website that adapts to the specific needs of the user. Machine learning can identify the intention of the user for visiting the website and can adapt the information as well as the design of the website to satisfy the user's needs.

3. Agriculture

Almost every sector can benefit from machine learning and that includes the agriculture sector, an industry you don't typically associate with advanced technology. The agriculture sector is always looking for information on how certain crops perform in different climates and conditions. This can take decades of collecting data and a million combinations to find the set of genes that would be best for the type of crop they are growing. Machine learning can narrow down this data and create a digital test to know how a certain crop might perform in certain types of soil, weather conditions, and plant diseases. This is not a perfect prediction; however, breeders now have more information and a thorough examination of conditions before planting the crop or developing a product.

4. Credit Card Fraud

With the rise of mobile phones in recent years, more people have access to the internet. This coincides with the growth of online shopping and e-commerce. Unfortunately, this also means the rise of credit card frauds. The good news for most credit card providers is they already have the data credit card frauds. They can combine this with the shopping behavior of the credit card holder and detect anomalies as well as patterns on fraudulent behavior.

Credit card frauds are not just increasing, scammers are also using different tricks and increasing the variety of credit card scams. They are getting more advanced and adapting to the technology of our time. This is another reason to use machine learning. A computer system that continuously learns and collects data to improve the system is an excellent way to counter financial fraud that adapts with modern technology.

5. Computational Linguistics

Computational linguistics is evaluating and integrating computers with human language. One of the main goals of this field is to have humans interact with computers as if they are communicating with people. Alexa Voice, Siri, and Google Assistant is in the infancy stage of this technology. Machine learning on computational linguistics will have a variety of applications which includes instant language translation, analyzing language for context, voice to text, text to speech, and creating chatbots for sales and customer service.

Basically it is having the computer learn the human language instead of the current state wherein people have to learn the language of the computer to use it. Computational linguistics is one sector that need the continuous learning aspect of machine learning. Computers have to learn every major language at the very least and they have to be tailored to specific industries and institutions as well as the specific needs of an user.

6. Machine Perception

This is the ability of a computer to use senses, including vision, hearing, and touch, to interpret the world around them. Machine learning will be combined with the traditional way of humans inputting data into the computer and using all that information for accuracy and efficiency.

The field of research will have one of the best applications for machine perception and machine learning. The machine will learn research skills combined with sensory input to interpret data. This will benefit the fields of research that are dangerous for humans such as infrared, radiation, deep see exploration, and outer space.

7. Fiction Writing

Even creative fields can find a use for machine learning. For example, Wattpad is a popular website for fiction writers and readers. In 2018 they ran a contest where the writer interacts with an AI chatbot to create a story.

Fiction writing is an art and a science. The most successful films and novels use a story structure to put the creativity of the writer into a framework. Machine learning can master the common story structures and put it in software that a human writer can use to keep his imagination and grammar intact.

8. Health Care

The application of **machine learning** for healthcare is detecting patients with deteriorating health long before they need hospitalization. The aim of the health care industry is precision particularly in the early detection of terminal diseases like cancer, AIDS, heart disease, and diabetes. Detecting a disease sooner can save lives.

9. More Efficient Energy Use

Machine learning can be used to predict energy load. This means more efficient use of energy, lesser cost, less waste, and maximizing peak demand. Machine learning can also be used to research sustainable and renewable energy and how it will impact several industries which still relies on nonrenewable energy sources like crude oil, coal, and natural gas.

Machine learning can truly benefit many sectors and industries. But the most important factor is how it can benefit individuals and ordinary families. Industries, governments, and ordinary people have to be vigilant and responsible so that this technology will be used to benefit majority of the world and not just a few sectors that will gain much of the upside.

Chapter 13: The Machine Learning Toolbox

As you learn more about machine learning (or ML for short) you should want to try your hand at being a developer. If you're the manager of a business and you have now realized how machine learning can help give your enterprise a boost, then you will want your staff to be properly equipped with the best tools. That is actually the next logical step for both developer and enterprise head.

Of course, not all tools are built the same. On top of that it is also important to have the best tools to work with the most beneficial algorithms. In this chapter we'll go over the factors that you should consider when selecting the right tools and also a few recommended tools along the way.

Why Use Machine Learning Tools

You don't have to reinvent the wheel per se, right? The same is true in machine learning. Tools were envisioned and created to obtain certain advantages, such as the following:

- *They make the work faster*: you can use ML tools to automate parts of the development process.
- *They make things a lot easier*: you don't spend a lot of time and use a lot of technical expertise to make sure that the process is applied efficiently.
- *Reduces the learning curve*: beginners get to see the results faster. They get to practice with more models and projects and learn lessons from each one of them.

Get the Best Tools

Tools for machine learning are more than just simple implementations of the many different algorithms already described in this book. They empower your business with capabilities to efficiently solve issues within your industry.

But how can you tell which tool is best suited for you? Here are several factors that should influence your choice:

- *Best Practice*: there is already a growing body of best practices that are being set for the development and implementation of machine learning tools. These include tool structure as well as automatic configurations.

- *Intuitive Interface*: an intuitive interface has become the standard in machine learning tools. There should be good mapping so that the interface is best suited for the necessary subtasks.

- *Available Support*: the best machine learning tools are the ones that are used the most. The more people trust and use a tool the more you know that it is a really good choice. There should be a community of people talking about it, sharing their tips and tricks and also a lot of available support from the maker of the tool.

Platforms and Libraries

You can classify machine learning tools into general use tools and specific purpose tools. For instance, some tools are just libraries for specific tasks—thus you can classify that as a specific purpose tool. Some ML tools on the other hand are complete platforms, which you can say are general use tools.

Examples of ML platform tools are scikit learn and Pandas from Python SciPy, R Platform, and WEKA Machine Learning Workbench. Examples of specific or library tools are GoLearn (local tool), Microsoft Azure Machine Learning (remote tool), and MLlib (library).

However, this distinction can be blurred as some libraries are quite extensive and can be used for every phase in development. There are also platforms that have specialized tools suited for specific tasks.

ML Platforms

ML platforms give you a comprehensive set of tools that can help you with projects from beginning to end. They have the following features:

- Tailored for general purpose use
- They aren't designed for scalability or speed
- They have loose coupling features—that means you have to define the specifics when tying pieces together.

- Interfaces can be command line, graphical, or a combination of both
- There is a suite of features and capabilities that you can use for each phase of project development

Remote and Local Tools

These two classifications are for specific tools. A local tool is one that you store in a local computer and isn't shared in a network. A remote tool is shared and is network based or cloud based.

Local tools have the following features:

- They integrate into any system that you're developing
- They give you control over parameters and configurations
- They're better suited for in-memory algorithms and data

Remote tools on the other hand have the following features:

- They can be used for scaled and large data sets
- They work with remote procedure calls to get integrated into local environments
- Fewer algorithms
- They can be run across multiple systems
- Simpler interfaces
- They can be used to setup custom remote solutions
- They can be integrated into environments as a service

Sample Tools

The following are some of the best machine learning tools that we recommend.

- **Google ML Kit**

This is Google's very own machine learning offering, never expect them to be behind in any tech race. This tool kit is best suited for developers and those who want to learn how to machine learning features for mobile devices running iOS, and Android etc.

It's a good option for anyone at any level from absolute beginner to a total expert. Some of the use cases that can be developed include landmark recognition, image labelling, barcode scanning, face detection, and text recognition.

- **Apache Mahout**

This tool is best suited for data scientists and statisticians. It's actually a distributed linear algebra framework. It allows you to implement your very own custom built algorithms. It has scalable implementation and it caters to specific areas such as classification, collaborative filtering, and clustering among others.

- **OpenNN**

If you're into C++ programming then this might be a good option for you. It's actually a programming library. It is primarily designed for C++ programmers who already have some experience with machine learning. If you are looking to develop neural networks using this programming language then this is a pretty good option for you.

- **Accord.net Framework**

This tool is open source, which means it's free. It's a framework for .net, which should be obvious. Included in the pack is a set of libraries that can be used for processing image streams and audio signals. Its algorithms are suited for tasks such as tracking moving objects, face recognition, putting images together, and vision processing.

More Than A Thousand Options

There are actually thousands of ML tools out there. Do a simple Google search and you will be overwhelmed with the search results. You can of course start with open source tools so you don't have to spend a dime. Do your own research into other tools available and spend your money wisely on tools that fit your machine learning projects nicely.

Conclusion

I would like to thank you once more for downloading this book.

It is my hope that you have benefitted immensely from what you have learned. The next step is to enter the foray of machine learning's more technical underpinnings and also discover how this growing technology can help you succeed in your business or career.

You can pursue several objectives. For instance, today machine learning is used as one of the quick solutions to solve a lot of finite business problems. Its potential is vast and there is no question about it. It may be just a bunch of business tools today but the way forward is into its many untapped areas.

Machine learning is currently gaining a lot of popularity in the global business community. The goal is to equip managers and other front line personnel with the right tools to make accurate decisions and recommendations for certain issues such as improving the customer's experience, resolving transaction conflicts, supply chain, and others.

The main power of machine learning is in its self-teaching algorithms. Part of this self-teaching feature is already being utilized in businesses today. Examples of which include the prediction of possible cancer cases as it is utilized in IBM Watson's Oncology as well as in Facebook's face recognition tool.

As you realize the potential of this technology, the opportunity to take advantage of this technology is yours. Fortune favors the bold as the Romans would say.

Thank you again for downloading this book.

www.ingramcontent.com/pod-product-compliance
Lightning Source LLC
Chambersburg PA
CBHW070858070326
40690CB00009B/1895